MznLnx

Missing Links Exam Preps

Exam Prep for

Managing Innovation: Integrating Technological, Market and Organizational Change

Tidd, Bessant & Pavitt, 3rd Edition

The MznLnx Exam Prep is your link from the texbook and lecture to your exams.
The MznLnx Exam Preps are unauthorized and comprehensive reviews of your textbooks.

All material provided by MznLnx and Rico Publications (c) 2010
Textbook publishers and textbook authors do not particpate in or contribute to these reviews.

MznLnx

Rico
Publications

Exam Prep for Managing Innovation: Integrating Technological, Market and Organizational Change
3rd Edition
Tidd, Bessant & Pavitt

Publisher: Raymond Houge
Assistant Editor: Michael Rouger
Text and Cover Designer: Lisa Buckner
Marketing Manager: Sara Swagger
Project Manager, Editorial Production: Jerry Emerson
Art Director: Vernon Lowerui
Product Manager: Dave Mason
Editorial Assitant: Rachel Guzmanji
Pedagogy: Debra Long
Cover Image: Jim Reed/Getty Images
Text and Cover Printer: City Printing, Inc.
Compositor: Media Mix, Inc.

(c) 2010 Rico Publications
ALL RIGHTS RESERVED. No part of this work covered by the copyright may be reproduced or used in any form or by an means--graphic, electronic, or mechanical, including photocopying, recording, taping, Web distribution, information storage, and retrieval systems, or in any other manner--without the written permission of the publisher.

Printed in the United States
ISBN:

For more information about our products, contact us at:
Dave.Mason@RicoPublications.com

For permission to use material from this text or product, submit a request online to:
Dave.Mason@RicoPublications.com

Contents

TO THE STUDENT

COMPREHENSIVE

The *MznLnx* Exam Prep series is designed to help you pass your exams. Editors at MznLnx review your textbooks and then prepare these practice exams to help you master the textbook material. Unlike study guides, workbooks, and practice tests provided by the texbook publisher and textbook authors, *MznLnx* gives you ***all*** of the material in each chapter in exam form, not just samples, so you can be sure to nail your exam.

MECHANICAL

The MznLnx Exam Prep series creates exams that will help you learn the subject matter as well as test you on your understanding. Each question is designed to help you master the concept. Just working through the exams, you gain an understanding of the subject--its a simple mechanical process that produces success.

INTEGRATED STUDY GUIDE AND REVIEW

MznLnx is not just a set of exams designed to test you, its also a comprehensive review of the subject content. Each exam question is also a review of the concept, making sure that you will get the answer correct without having to go to other sources of material. You learn as you go! Its the easiest way to pass an exam.

HUMOR

Studying can be tedious and dry. MznLnx's instructional design includes moderate humor within the exam questions on occassion, to break the tedium and revitalize the brain

1. _________ is, in very basic words, a position a firm occupies against its competitors.

According to Michael Porter, the three methods for creating a sustainable _________ are through:

1. Cost leadership

2. Differentiation

3. Focus (economics)

a. 1990 Clean Air Act
b. 28-hour day
c. Competitive advantage
d. Theory Z

2. _________ is an advertisement in which a particular product specifically mentions a competitor by name for the express purpose of showing why the competitor is inferior to the product naming it.

This should not be confused with parody advertisements, where a fictional product is being advertised for the purpose of poking fun at the particular advertisement, nor should it be confused with the use of a coined brand name for the purpose of comparing the product without actually naming an actual competitor. ('Wikipedia tastes better and is less filling than the Encyclopedia Galactica.')

In the 1980s, during what has been referred to as the cola wars, soft-drink manufacturer Pepsi ran a series of advertisements where people, caught on hidden camera, in a blind taste test, chose Pepsi over rival Coca-Cola.

a. 1990 Clean Air Act
b. 28-hour day
c. 33 Strategies of War
d. Comparative advertising

3. In commerce, _________ is the length of time it takes from a product being conceived until its being available for sale. _________ is important in industries where products are outmoded quickly. A common assumption is that _________ matters most for first-of-a-kind products, but actually the leader often has the luxury of time, while the clock is clearly running for the followers.

a. Market entry
b. Procurement
c. Time to market
d. Career development

4. Procter is a surname, and may also refer to:

- Bryan Waller Procter (pseud. Barry Cornwall), English poet
- Goodwin Procter, American law firm
- _________, consumer products multinational

.

a. Strict liability
b. Master and Servant Acts
c. Procter ' Gamble
d. Downstream

5. The process of _________ involves the introduction of a good or service that is new or substantially improved. This includes, but is not limited to, improvements in functional characteristics, technical abilities, or ease of use.
a. Product innovation
b. Letter of resignation
c. Service-profit chain
d. Job enlargement

6. The term _________ refers to a graphical representation of the 'average' rate of learning for an activity or tool. It can represent at a glance the initial difficulty of learning something and, to an extent, how much there is to learn after initial familiarity. For example, the Windows program Notepad is extremely simple to learn, but offers little after this.
a. Learning curve
b. 1990 Clean Air Act
c. 33 Strategies of War
d. 28-hour day

7. A _________ is the belief that there is a technique, method, process, activity, incentive or reward that is more effective at delivering a particular outcome than any other technique, method, process, etc. The idea is that with proper processes, checks, and testing, a desired outcome can be delivered with fewer problems and unforeseen complications. _________s can also be defined as the most efficient (least amount of effort) and effective (best results) way of accomplishing a task, based on repeatable procedures that have proven themselves over time for large numbers of people.
a. Fix it twice
b. Design management
c. Best practice
d. Hierarchical organization

8. _________ are legal property rights over creations of the mind, both artistic and commercial, and the corresponding fields of law. Under _________ law, owners are granted certain exclusive rights to a variety of intangible assets, such as musical, literary, and artistic works; ideas, discoveries and inventions; and words, phrases, symbols, and designs. Common types of _________ include copyrights, trademarks, patents, industrial design rights and trade secrets.

a. Unemployment Action Center
b. Intent
c. Equal Pay Act
d. Intellectual property

9. _________ plant, and equipment, is a term used in accountancy for assets and property which cannot easily be converted into cash. This can be compared with current assets such as cash or bank accounts, which are described as liquid assets. In most cases, only tangible assets are referred to as fixed.

a. 28-hour day
b. 1990 Clean Air Act
c. 33 Strategies of War
d. Fixed asset

10. _________ in its literal sense is the process of transformation of local or regional phenomena into global ones. It can be described as a process by which the people of the world are unified into a single society and function together.

This process is a combination of economic, technological, sociocultural and political forces.

a. Histogram
b. Collaborative Planning, Forecasting and Replenishment
c. Cost Management
d. Globalization

11. A _________ is a set of exclusive rights granted by a state to an inventor or his assignee for a limited period of time in exchange for a disclosure of an invention.

The procedure for granting _________s, the requirements placed on the _________ee and the extent of the exclusive rights vary widely between countries according to national laws and international agreements. Typically, however, a _________ application must include one or more claims defining the invention which must be new, inventive, and useful or industrially applicable.

a. Food, Drug, and Cosmetic Act
b. Labor Management Reporting and Disclosure Act
c. Federal Trade Commission Act
d. Patent

1. In business and engineering, _________ is the term used to describe the complete process of bringing a new product or service to market. There are two parallel paths involved in the _________ process: one involves the idea generation, product design, and detail engineering; the other involves market research and marketing analysis. Companies typically see _________ as the first stage in generating and commercializing new products within the overall strategic process of product life cycle management used to maintain or grow their market share.
   a. 28-hour day
   b. 33 Strategies of War
   c. 1990 Clean Air Act
   d. New product development

2. _________ is subcontracting a process, such as product design or manufacturing, to a third-party company. The decision to outsource is often made in the interest of lowering cost or making better use of time and energy costs, redirecting or conserving energy directed at the competencies of a particular business, or to make more efficient use of land, labor, capital, (information) technology and resources. _________ became part of the business lexicon during the 1980s.
   a. Opinion leadership
   b. Unemployment insurance
   c. Outsourcing
   d. Operant conditioning

3. In business and engineering, new _________ is the term used to describe the complete process of bringing a new product or service to market. There are two parallel paths involved in the NProduct development process: one involves the idea generation, product design, and detail engineering; the other involves market research and marketing analysis. Companies typically see new _________ as the first stage in generating and commercializing new products within the overall strategic process of product life cycle management used to maintain or grow their market share.
   a. 1990 Clean Air Act
   b. 28-hour day
   c. Product development
   d. 33 Strategies of War

4. _________ is an advertisement in which a particular product specifically mentions a competitor by name for the express purpose of showing why the competitor is inferior to the product naming it.

This should not be confused with parody advertisements, where a fictional product is being advertised for the purpose of poking fun at the particular advertisement, nor should it be confused with the use of a coined brand name for the purpose of comparing the product without actually naming an actual competitor. ('Wikipedia tastes better and is less filling than the Encyclopedia Galactica.')

In the 1980s, during what has been referred to as the cola wars, soft-drink manufacturer Pepsi ran a series of advertisements where people, caught on hidden camera, in a blind taste test, chose Pepsi over rival Coca-Cola.

a. 33 Strategies of War
b. 1990 Clean Air Act
c. 28-hour day
d. Comparative advertising

5. _________ of the learning curve effect and the closely related experience curve effect express the relationship between equations for experience and efficiency or between efficiency gains and investment in the effort. The experience of 'learning curves' was first observed by the 19th Century German psychologist Hermann Ebbinghaus according to the difficulty of memorizing varying numbers of verbal stimuli, and subsequent learning about the complex processes of learning are discussed in the

.

The rule used for representing the learning curve effect states that the more times a task has been performed, the less time will be required on each subsequent iteration.

a. Spatial Decision Support Systems
b. Distribution
c. Point biserial correlation coefficient
d. Models

6. Procter is a surname, and may also refer to:

- Bryan Waller Procter (pseud. Barry Cornwall), English poet
- Goodwin Procter, American law firm
- _________, consumer products multinational

.

a. Master and Servant Acts
b. Strict liability
c. Downstream
d. Procter ' Gamble

7. _________ is the process of comparing the cost, cycle time, productivity, or quality of a specific process or method to another that is widely considered to be an industry standard or best practice. Essentially, _________ provides a snapshot of the performance of your business and helps you understand where you are in relation to a particular standard. The result is often a business case for making changes in order to make improvements.

a. Complementors
b. Competitive heterogeneity
c. Cost leadership
d. Benchmarking

8. A _________ is the belief that there is a technique, method, process, activity, incentive or reward that is more effective at delivering a particular outcome than any other technique, method, process, etc. The idea is that with proper processes, checks, and testing, a desired outcome can be delivered with fewer problems and unforeseen complications. _________s can also be defined as the most efficient (least amount of effort) and effective (best results) way of accomplishing a task, based on repeatable procedures that have proven themselves over time for large numbers of people.
a. Design management
b. Hierarchical organization
c. Fix it twice
d. Best practice

9. A _________ is a volunteer group composed of workers (or even students), usually under the leadership of their supervisor (but they can elect a team leader), who are trained to identify, analyse and solve work-related problems and present their solutions to management in order to improve the performance of the organization, and motivate and enrich the work of employees. When matured, true _________s become self-managing, having gained the confidence of management. _________s are an alternative to the dehumanising concept of the Division of Labour, where workers or individuals are treated like robots.
a. Certified in Production and Inventory Management
b. Competency-based job descriptions
c. Connectionist expert systems
d. Quality circle

10. A _________ is a set of exclusive rights granted by a state to an inventor or his assignee for a limited period of time in exchange for a disclosure of an invention.

The procedure for granting _________s, the requirements placed on the _________ee and the extent of the exclusive rights vary widely between countries according to national laws and international agreements. Typically, however, a _________ application must include one or more claims defining the invention which must be new, inventive, and useful or industrially applicable.

a. Federal Trade Commission Act
b. Patent
c. Food, Drug, and Cosmetic Act
d. Labor Management Reporting and Disclosure Act

11. In marketing, _________ has come to mean the process by which marketers try to create an image or identity in the minds of their target market for its product, brand, or organization. It is the 'relative competitive comparison' their product occupies in a given market as perceived by the target market.

Re-_________ involves changing the identity of a product, relative to the identity of competing products, in the collective minds of the target market.

a. Positioning
b. Context analysis
c. Customer analytics
d. PEST analysis

1. _________ is a strategic planning method used to evaluate the Strengths, Weaknesses, Opportunities, and Threats involved in a project or in a business venture. It involves specifying the objective of the business venture or project and identifying the internal and external factors that are favorable and unfavorable to achieving that objective. The technique is credited to Albert Humphrey, who led a convention at Stanford University in the 1960s and 1970s using data from Fortune 500 companies.

a. Market share
b. Corporate image
c. Marketing
d. SWOT analysis

2. _________ is the process of estimation in unknown situations. Prediction is a similar, but more general term. Both can refer to estimation of time series, cross-sectional or longitudinal data.

a. 33 Strategies of War
b. 28-hour day
c. 1990 Clean Air Act
d. Forecasting

3. _________ is something that a firm can do well and that meets the following three conditions:

Competencies are things that companys execute well across several business units or product sectors.

Firms usually have few competencies, but these are usually less liable to change rapidly.

1. It provides consumer benefits
2. It is not easy for competitors to imitate
3. It can be leveraged widely to many products and markets.

A _________ can take various forms, including technical/subject matter know-how, a reliable process and/or close relationships with customers and suppliers (Mascarenhas et al. 1998.)

a. NAIRU
b. Core competency
c. Dominant Design
d. Learning-by-doing

4. _________ has been described as the 'process of social influence in which one person can enlist the aid and support of others in the accomplishment of a common task' . A definition more inclusive of followers comes from Alan Keith of Genentech who said '_________ is ultimately about creating a way for people to contribute to making something extraordinary happen.'

_________ is one of the most salient aspects of the organizational context. However, defining _________ has been challenging.

a. 28-hour day
b. 1990 Clean Air Act
c. Situational leadership
d. Leadership

5. In marketing, _________ has come to mean the process by which marketers try to create an image or identity in the minds of their target market for its product, brand, or organization. It is the 'relative competitive comparison' their product occupies in a given market as perceived by the target market.

Re-_________ involves changing the identity of a product, relative to the identity of competing products, in the collective minds of the target market.

a. Context analysis
b. PEST analysis
c. Customer analytics
d. Positioning

1. _________ in its literal sense is the process of transformation of local or regional phenomena into global ones. It can be described as a process by which the people of the world are unified into a single society and function together.

This process is a combination of economic, technological, sociocultural and political forces.

a. Globalization
b. Cost Management
c. Histogram
d. Collaborative Planning, Forecasting and Replenishment

2. In economics, _________ is the desire to own something and the ability to pay for it. The term _________ signifies the ability or the willingness to buy a particular commodity at a given point of time.
a. Demand
b. 33 Strategies of War
c. 1990 Clean Air Act
d. 28-hour day

3. _________ is the process of comparing the cost, cycle time, productivity, or quality of a specific process or method to another that is widely considered to be an industry standard or best practice. Essentially, _________ provides a snapshot of the performance of your business and helps you understand where you are in relation to a particular standard. The result is often a business case for making changes in order to make improvements.
a. Benchmarking
b. Complementors
c. Competitive heterogeneity
d. Cost leadership

4. _________ or lean production, which is often known simply as 'Lean', is a production practice that considers the expenditure of resources for any goal other than the creation of value for the end customer to be wasteful, and thus a target for elimination. Working from the perspective of the customer who consumes a product or service, 'value' is defined as any action or process that a customer would be willing to pay for. Basically, lean is centered around creating more value with less work.
a. Production line
b. Six Sigma
c. Lean manufacturing
d. Theory of constraints

5. A _________ is a set of exclusive rights granted by a state to an inventor or his assignee for a limited period of time in exchange for a disclosure of an invention.

The procedure for granting _________s, the requirements placed on the _________ee and the extent of the exclusive rights vary widely between countries according to national laws and international agreements. Typically, however, a _________ application must include one or more claims defining the invention which must be new, inventive, and useful or industrially applicable.

a. Federal Trade Commission Act
b. Food, Drug, and Cosmetic Act
c. Labor Management Reporting and Disclosure Act
d. Patent

6. _________ has been described as the 'process of social influence in which one person can enlist the aid and support of others in the accomplishment of a common task' . A definition more inclusive of followers comes from Alan Keith of Genentech who said '_________ is ultimately about creating a way for people to contribute to making something extraordinary happen.'

_________ is one of the most salient aspects of the organizational context. However, defining _________ has been challenging.

a. 1990 Clean Air Act
b. 28-hour day
c. Situational leadership
d. Leadership

7. A _________ is the period of time between the initiation of any process of production and the completion of that process. Thus the _________ for ordering a new car from a manufacturer may be anywhere from 2 weeks to 6 months. In industry, _________ reduction is an important part of lean manufacturing.

a. 33 Strategies of War
b. 1990 Clean Air Act
c. 28-hour day
d. Lead time

8. The term _________ refers to a graphical representation of the 'average' rate of learning for an activity or tool. It can represent at a glance the initial difficulty of learning something and, to an extent, how much there is to learn after initial familiarity. For example, the Windows program Notepad is extremely simple to learn, but offers little after this.

a. 33 Strategies of War
b. 1990 Clean Air Act
c. 28-hour day
d. Learning curve

9. _________ is an advertisement in which a particular product specifically mentions a competitor by name for the express purpose of showing why the competitor is inferior to the product naming it.

This should not be confused with parody advertisements, where a fictional product is being advertised for the purpose of poking fun at the particular advertisement, nor should it be confused with the use of a coined brand name for the purpose of comparing the product without actually naming an actual competitor. ('Wikipedia tastes better and is less filling than the Encyclopedia Galactica.')

In the 1980s, during what has been referred to as the cola wars, soft-drink manufacturer Pepsi ran a series of advertisements where people, caught on hidden camera, in a blind taste test, chose Pepsi over rival Coca-Cola.

a. 1990 Clean Air Act
b. 28-hour day
c. Comparative advertising
d. 33 Strategies of War

10. Procter is a surname, and may also refer to:

- Bryan Waller Procter (pseud. Barry Cornwall), English poet
- Goodwin Procter, American law firm
- _________, consumer products multinational

a. Strict liability
b. Procter ' Gamble
c. Downstream
d. Master and Servant Acts

11. _________ are legal property rights over creations of the mind, both artistic and commercial, and the corresponding fields of law. Under _________ law, owners are granted certain exclusive rights to a variety of intangible assets, such as musical, literary, and artistic works; ideas, discoveries and inventions; and words, phrases, symbols, and designs. Common types of _________ include copyrights, trademarks, patents, industrial design rights and trade secrets.

a. Equal Pay Act
b. Intent
c. Unemployment Action Center
d. Intellectual property

12. _________ plant, and equipment, is a term used in accountancy for assets and property which cannot easily be converted into cash. This can be compared with current assets such as cash or bank accounts, which are described as liquid assets. In most cases, only tangible assets are referred to as fixed.
a. 33 Strategies of War
b. 28-hour day
c. 1990 Clean Air Act
d. Fixed asset

13. _________ is technology based on biology, especially when used in agriculture, food science, and medicine. United Nations Convention on Biological Diversity defines _________ as:

_________ is often used to refer to genetic engineering technology of the 21st century, however the term encompasses a wider range and history of procedures for modifying biological organisms according to the needs of humanity, going back to the initial modifications of native plants into improved food crops through artificial selection and hybridization. Bioengineering is the science upon which all biotechnological applications are based.

a. 28-hour day
b. Biotechnology
c. 33 Strategies of War
d. 1990 Clean Air Act

1. Procter is a surname, and may also refer to:

- Bryan Waller Procter (pseud. Barry Cornwall), English poet
- Goodwin Procter, American law firm
- _________, consumer products multinational

.

a. Master and Servant Acts
b. Downstream
c. Procter ' Gamble
d. Strict liability

2. A _________ is a process in which a potential employee is evaluated by an employer for prospective employment in their company, organization and was established in the late 16th century.

A _________ typically precedes the hiring decision, and is used to evaluate the candidate. The interview is usually preceded by the evaluation of submitted résumés from interested candidates, then selecting a small number of candidates for interviews.

a. Supported employment
b. Job interview
c. Split shift
d. Payrolling

3. _________ is technology based on biology, especially when used in agriculture, food science, and medicine. United Nations Convention on Biological Diversity defines _________ as:

_________ is often used to refer to genetic engineering technology of the 21st century, however the term encompasses a wider range and history of procedures for modifying biological organisms according to the needs of humanity, going back to the initial modifications of native plants into improved food crops through artificial selection and hybridization. Bioengineering is the science upon which all biotechnological applications are based.

a. 33 Strategies of War
b. 1990 Clean Air Act
c. Biotechnology
d. 28-hour day

4. _________ is something that a firm can do well and that meets the following three conditions:

Competencies are things that companys execute well across several business units or product sectors.

Firms usually have few competencies, but these are usually less liable to change rapidly.

1. It provides consumer benefits
2. It is not easy for competitors to imitate
3. It can be leveraged widely to many products and markets.

A _________ can take various forms, including technical/subject matter know-how, a reliable process and/or close relationships with customers and suppliers (Mascarenhas et al. 1998.)

a. Dominant Design
b. Learning-by-doing
c. NAIRU
d. Core competency

5. A _________ researches, selects, develops, and places a company's products.

A _________ considers numerous factors such as target demographic, the products offered by the competition, and how well the product fits in with the company's business model. Generally, a _________ manages one or more tangible products.

a. 28-hour day
b. 33 Strategies of War
c. 1990 Clean Air Act
d. Product manager

6. _________ is the use of control systems (such as numerical control, programmable logic control, and other industrial control systems), in concert with other applications of information technology (such as computer-aided technologies [CAD, CAM, CAx]), to control industrial machinery and processes, reducing the need for human intervention. In the scope of industrialization, _________ is a step beyond mechanization. Whereas mechanization provided human operators with machinery to assist them with the physical requirements of work, _________ greatly reduces the need for human sensory and mental requirements as well.

a. A Stake in the Outcome
b. AAAI
c. A4e
d. Automation

1. A _________ is a process in which a potential employee is evaluated by an employer for prospective employment in their company, organization and was established in the late 16th century.

A _________ typically precedes the hiring decision, and is used to evaluate the candidate. The interview is usually preceded by the evaluation of submitted résumés from interested candidates, then selecting a small number of candidates for interviews.

a. Split shift
b. Payrolling
c. Supported employment
d. Job interview

2. _________ in its literal sense is the process of transformation of local or regional phenomena into global ones. It can be described as a process by which the people of the world are unified into a single society and function together.

This process is a combination of economic, technological, sociocultural and political forces.

a. Histogram
b. Cost Management
c. Collaborative Planning, Forecasting and Replenishment
d. Globalization

3. _________ is technology based on biology, especially when used in agriculture, food science, and medicine. United Nations Convention on Biological Diversity defines _________ as:

_________ is often used to refer to genetic engineering technology of the 21st century, however the term encompasses a wider range and history of procedures for modifying biological organisms according to the needs of humanity, going back to the initial modifications of native plants into improved food crops through artificial selection and hybridization. Bioengineering is the science upon which all biotechnological applications are based.

a. 1990 Clean Air Act
b. Biotechnology
c. 33 Strategies of War
d. 28-hour day

4. _________ is used to assign the available resources in an economic way. It is part of resource management.

In strategic planning,is a plan for using available resources, for example human resources, especially in the near term, to achieve goals for the future.

a. Resource allocation
b. 1990 Clean Air Act
c. 33 Strategies of War
d. 28-hour day

5. _________ or net present worth (NPW) is defined as the total present value (PV) of a time series of cash flows. It is a standard method for using the time value of money to appraise long-term projects. Used for capital budgeting, and widely throughout economics, it measures the excess or shortfall of cash flows, in present value terms, once financing charges are met.

a. Present value
b. Net present value
c. Discounted cash flow
d. 1990 Clean Air Act

6. _________ is the value on a given date of a future payment or series of future payments, discounted to reflect the time value of money and other factors such as investment risk. _________ calculations are widely used in business and economics to provide a means to compare cash flows at different times on a meaningful 'like to like' basis.

If offered a choice between $100 today or $100 in one year, everyone will choose $100 today.

a. Net present value
b. Discounted cash flow
c. Present value
d. 1990 Clean Air Act

7. In marketing, _________ has come to mean the process by which marketers try to create an image or identity in the minds of their target market for its product, brand, or organization. It is the 'relative competitive comparison' their product occupies in a given market as perceived by the target market.

Re-_________ involves changing the identity of a product, relative to the identity of competing products, in the collective minds of the target market.

a. Customer analytics
b. PEST analysis
c. Positioning
d. Context analysis

8. _________ is one of the managerial functions like planning, organizing, staffing and directing. It is an important function because it helps to check the errors and to take the corrective action so that deviation from standards are minimized and stated goals of the organization are achieved in desired manner.According to modern concepts, _________ is a foreseeing action whereas earlier concept of _________ was used only when errors were detected. _________ in management means setting standards, measuring actual performance and taking corrective action.

a. Control
b. Turnover
c. Schedule of reinforcement
d. Decision tree pruning

9. _________ according to Onuoha (2007) is the practice of starting new organizations or revitalizing mature organizations, particularly new businesses generally in response to identified opportunities. _________ is often a difficult undertaking, as a vast majority of new businesses fail. Entrepreneurial activities are substantially different depending on the type of organization that is being started.

a. A4e
b. A Stake in the Outcome
c. AAAI
d. Entrepreneurship

1. _________ is the process by which a new idea or new product is accepted by the market. The rate of _________ is the speed that the new idea spreads from one consumer to the next. Adoption is similar to _________ except that it deals with the psychological processes an individual goes through, rather than an aggregate market process.

a. Value chain
b. Category management
c. Diffusion
d. Mass marketing

2. Procter is a surname, and may also refer to:

- Bryan Waller Procter (pseud. Barry Cornwall), English poet
- Goodwin Procter, American law firm
- _________, consumer products multinational

.

a. Downstream
b. Master and Servant Acts
c. Strict liability
d. Procter ' Gamble

3. _________ can be considered to have three main components: quality control, quality assurance and quality improvement. _________ is focused not only on product quality, but also the means to achieve it. _________ therefore uses quality assurance and control of processes as well as products to achieve more consistent quality.

a. 1990 Clean Air Act
b. Quality management
c. 28-hour day
d. Total quality management

4. _________ is a broad label that refers to any individuals or households that use goods and services generated within the economy. The concept of a _________ is used in different contexts, so that the usage and significance of the term may vary.

Typically when business people and economists talk of _________s they are talking about person as _________, an aggregated commodity item with little individuality other than that expressed in the buy/not-buy decision.

a. Consumer
b. 1990 Clean Air Act
c. 33 Strategies of War
d. 28-hour day

5. _________ is an integrated communications-based process through which individuals and communities discover that existing and newly-identified needs and wants may be satisfied by the products and services of others.

_________ is defined by the American _________ Association as the activity, set of institutions, and processes for creating, communicating, delivering, and exchanging offerings that have value for customers, clients, partners, and society at large. The term developed from the original meaning which referred literally to going to market, as in shopping, or going to a market to buy or sell goods or services.

a. Market development
b. Disruptive technology
c. Customer relationship management
d. Marketing

6. _________ is an advertisement in which a particular product specifically mentions a competitor by name for the express purpose of showing why the competitor is inferior to the product naming it.

This should not be confused with parody advertisements, where a fictional product is being advertised for the purpose of poking fun at the particular advertisement, nor should it be confused with the use of a coined brand name for the purpose of comparing the product without actually naming an actual competitor. ('Wikipedia tastes better and is less filling than the Encyclopedia Galactica.')

In the 1980s, during what has been referred to as the cola wars, soft-drink manufacturer Pepsi ran a series of advertisements where people, caught on hidden camera, in a blind taste test, chose Pepsi over rival Coca-Cola.

a. 33 Strategies of War
b. 28-hour day
c. 1990 Clean Air Act
d. Comparative advertising

7. _________ are legal property rights over creations of the mind, both artistic and commercial, and the corresponding fields of law. Under _________ law, owners are granted certain exclusive rights to a variety of intangible assets, such as musical, literary, and artistic works; ideas, discoveries and inventions; and words, phrases, symbols, and designs. Common types of _________ include copyrights, trademarks, patents, industrial design rights and trade secrets.

a. Unemployment Action Center
b. Intent
c. Equal Pay Act
d. Intellectual property

8. _________ plant, and equipment, is a term used in accountancy for assets and property which cannot easily be converted into cash. This can be compared with current assets such as cash or bank accounts, which are described as liquid assets. In most cases, only tangible assets are referred to as fixed.

a. 33 Strategies of War
b. 28-hour day
c. 1990 Clean Air Act
d. Fixed asset

9. A _________ is a set of exclusive rights granted by a state to an inventor or his assignee for a limited period of time in exchange for a disclosure of an invention.

The procedure for granting _________s, the requirements placed on the _________ee and the extent of the exclusive rights vary widely between countries according to national laws and international agreements. Typically, however, a _________ application must include one or more claims defining the invention which must be new, inventive, and useful or industrially applicable.

a. Federal Trade Commission Act
b. Food, Drug, and Cosmetic Act
c. Labor Management Reporting and Disclosure Act
d. Patent

10. _________ is one of the four Ps of the marketing mix. The other three aspects are product, promotion, and place. It is also a key variable in microeconomic price allocation theory.

a. Price floor
b. Transfer pricing
c. Pricing
d. Penetration pricing

11. In economics, business, retail, and accounting, a _________ is the value of money that has been used up to produce something, and hence is not available for use anymore. In economics, a _________ is an alternative that is given up as a result of a decision. In business, the _________ may be one of acquisition, in which case the amount of money expended to acquire it is counted as _________.

a. Fixed costs
b. Cost allocation
c. Cost
d. Cost overrun

12. _________ is a term developed by Eric von Hippel in 1986. His definition for _________ is:

1. _________s face needs that will be general in a marketplace - but face them months or years before the bulk of that marketplace encounters them, and
2. _________s are positioned to benefit significantly by obtaining a solution to those needs.

In other words: _________s are users of a product that currently experience needs still unknown to the public and who also benefit greatly if they obtain a solution to these needs.

The _________ Method is a market research tool that may be used by companies and / or individuals seeking to develop breakthrough products. _________ methodology was originally developed by Dr. Eric von Hippel of the Massachusetts Institute of Technology (MIT) and first described in the July 1986 issue of the Journal of Management Science.

a. 28-hour day
b. Lead user
c. 1990 Clean Air Act
d. 33 Strategies of War

13. _________ according to Onuoha (2007) is the practice of starting new organizations or revitalizing mature organizations, particularly new businesses generally in response to identified opportunities. _________ is often a difficult undertaking, as a vast majority of new businesses fail. Entrepreneurial activities are substantially different depending on the type of organization that is being started.

a. AAAI
b. A4e
c. A Stake in the Outcome
d. Entrepreneurship

14. An _________ is a person who has possession of an enterprise and assumes significant accountability for the inherent risks and the outcome. It is an ambitious leader who combines land, labor, and capital to create and market new goods or services. The term is a loanword from French and was first defined by the Irish economist Richard Cantillon.

a. A4e
b. A Stake in the Outcome
c. AAAI
d. Entrepreneur

15. _________ is the process of estimation in unknown situations. Prediction is a similar, but more general term. Both can refer to estimation of time series, cross-sectional or longitudinal data.
a. 28-hour day
b. 33 Strategies of War
c. 1990 Clean Air Act
d. Forecasting

16. _________ is the use of control systems (such as numerical control, programmable logic control, and other industrial control systems), in concert with other applications of information technology (such as computer-aided technologies [CAD, CAM, CAx]), to control industrial machinery and processes, reducing the need for human intervention. In the scope of industrialization, _________ is a step beyond mechanization. Whereas mechanization provided human operators with machinery to assist them with the physical requirements of work, _________ greatly reduces the need for human sensory and mental requirements as well.
a. Automation
b. AAAI
c. A Stake in the Outcome
d. A4e

17. _________ is a group creativity technique designed to generate a large number of ideas for the solution of a problem. The method was first popularized in the late 1930s by Alex Faickney Osborn in a book called Applied Imagination. Osborn proposed that groups could double their creative output with _________.
a. Affiliation
b. Abraham Harold Maslow
c. Brainstorming
d. Adam Smith

18. _________ is a strategic planning method that some organizations use to make flexible long-term plans. It is in large part an adaptation and generalization of classic methods used by military intelligence.

The original method was that a group of analysts would generate simulation games for policy makers. In business applications, the emphasis on gaming the behavior of opponents was reduced (shifting more toward a game against nature). At Royal Dutch/Shell for example, _________ was viewed as changing mindsets about the exogenous part of the world, prior to formulating specific strategies.

a. Time and attendance
b. Retroactive overtime
c. Labour productivity
d. Scenario planning

19. The _________ is a systematic, interactive forecasting method which relies on a panel of independent experts. The carefully selected experts answer questionnaires in two or more rounds. After each round, a facilitator provides an anonymous summary of the experts' forecasts from the previous round as well as the reasons they provided for their judgments.
a. Quality function deployment
b. Learning organization
c. Hoshin Kanri
d. Delphi method

1. The phrase mergers and _________s refers to the aspect of corporate strategy, corporate finance and management dealing with the buying, selling and combining of different companies that can aid, finance, or help a growing company in a given industry grow rapidly without having to create another business entity.

An _________, also known as a takeover or a buyout, is the buying of one company (the 'target') by another. An _________ may be friendly or hostile.

a. A4e
b. AAAI
c. A Stake in the Outcome
d. Acquisition

2. In economics, business, retail, and accounting, a _________ is the value of money that has been used up to produce something, and hence is not available for use anymore. In economics, a _________ is an alternative that is given up as a result of a decision. In business, the _________ may be one of acquisition, in which case the amount of money expended to acquire it is counted as _________.

a. Fixed costs
b. Cost overrun
c. Cost
d. Cost allocation

3. In economics and related disciplines, a _________ is a cost incurred in making an economic exchange. For example, most people, when buying or selling a stock, must pay a commission to their broker; that commission is a _________ of doing the stock deal. Or consider buying a banana from a store; to purchase the banana, your costs will be not only the price of the banana itself, but also the energy and effort it requires to find out which of the various banana products you prefer, where to get them and at what price, the cost of traveling from your house to the store and back, the time waiting in line, and the effort of the paying itself; the costs above and beyond the cost of the banana are the _________s.

a. Cost overrun
b. Transaction cost
c. Fixed costs
d. Cost accounting

4. _________ describes commerce transactions between businesses, such as between a manufacturer and a wholesaler, or between a wholesaler and a retailer. Contrasting terms are business-to-consumer (B2C) and business-to-government (B2G.)

The volume of B2B transactions is much higher than the volume of B2C transactions.

a. Product bundling
b. Market environment
c. Category management
d. Business-to-business

5. _________ or lean production, which is often known simply as 'Lean', is a production practice that considers the expenditure of resources for any goal other than the creation of value for the end customer to be wasteful, and thus a target for elimination. Working from the perspective of the customer who consumes a product or service, 'value' is defined as any action or process that a customer would be willing to pay for. Basically, lean is centered around creating more value with less work.
a. Six Sigma
b. Theory of constraints
c. Production line
d. Lean manufacturing

6. A _________ is a type of business entity in which partners (owners) share with each other the profits or losses of the business. _________s are often favored over corporations for taxation purposes, as the _________ structure does not generally incur a tax on profits before it is distributed to the partners (i.e. there is no dividend tax levied.) However, depending on the _________ structure and the jurisdiction in which it operates, owners of a _________ may be exposed to greater personal liability than they would as shareholders of a corporation.
a. Mediation
b. Federal Employers Liability Act
c. Due process
d. Partnership

7. A _________ is an entity formed between two or more parties to undertake economic activity together. The parties agree to create a new entity by both contributing equity, and they then share in the revenues, expenses, and control of the enterprise. The venture can be for one specific project only, or a continuing business relationship such as the Fuji Xerox _________.
a. Patent
b. Meritor Savings Bank v. Vinson
c. Joint venture
d. Civil Rights Act of 1991

8. An _________ is a person who has possession of an enterprise and assumes significant accountability for the inherent risks and the outcome. It is an ambitious leader who combines land, labor, and capital to create and market new goods or services. The term is a loanword from French and was first defined by the Irish economist Richard Cantillon.

a. A Stake in the Outcome
b. AAAI
c. A4e
d. Entrepreneur

9. A _________ is a set of companies with interlocking business relationships and shareholdings. It is a type of business group.

The prototypical _________ are those which appeared in Japan during the 'economic miracle' following World War II.

a. 33 Strategies of War
b. 1990 Clean Air Act
c. 28-hour day
d. Keiretsu

10. An _________ is a private computer network that uses Internet technologies to securely share any part of an organization's information or operational systems with its employees. Sometimes the term refers only to the organization's internal website, but often it is a more extensive part of the organization's computer infrastructure and private websites are an important component and focal point of internal communication and collaboration.

An _________ is built from the same concepts and technologies used for the Internet, such as client-server computing and the Internet Protocol Suite (TCP/IP.)

a. AAAI
b. Intranet
c. A Stake in the Outcome
d. A4e

11. _________ are legal property rights over creations of the mind, both artistic and commercial, and the corresponding fields of law. Under _________ law, owners are granted certain exclusive rights to a variety of intangible assets, such as musical, literary, and artistic works; ideas, discoveries and inventions; and words, phrases, symbols, and designs. Common types of _________ include copyrights, trademarks, patents, industrial design rights and trade secrets.

a. Unemployment Action Center
b. Intent
c. Intellectual property
d. Equal Pay Act

12. A _________ is a set of exclusive rights granted by a state to an inventor or his assignee for a limited period of time in exchange for a disclosure of an invention.

The procedure for granting _________s, the requirements placed on the _________ee and the extent of the exclusive rights vary widely between countries according to national laws and international agreements. Typically, however, a _________ application must include one or more claims defining the invention which must be new, inventive, and useful or industrially applicable.

a. Patent
b. Labor Management Reporting and Disclosure Act
c. Food, Drug, and Cosmetic Act
d. Federal Trade Commission Act

13. _________ plant, and equipment, is a term used in accountancy for assets and property which cannot easily be converted into cash. This can be compared with current assets such as cash or bank accounts, which are described as liquid assets. In most cases, only tangible assets are referred to as fixed.

a. 33 Strategies of War
b. 1990 Clean Air Act
c. 28-hour day
d. Fixed asset

14. _________ is something that a firm can do well and that meets the following three conditions:

Competencies are things that companys execute well across several business units or product sectors.

Firms usually have few competencies, but these are usually less liable to change rapidly.

1. It provides consumer benefits
2. It is not easy for competitors to imitate
3. It can be leveraged widely to many products and markets.

A _________ can take various forms, including technical/subject matter know-how, a reliable process and/or close relationships with customers and suppliers (Mascarenhas et al. 1998.)

a. Dominant Design
b. NAIRU
c. Core competency
d. Learning-by-doing

1. _________ of the learning curve effect and the closely related experience curve effect express the relationship between equations for experience and efficiency or between efficiency gains and investment in the effort. The experience of 'learning curves' was first observed by the 19th Century German psychologist Hermann Ebbinghaus according to the difficulty of memorizing varying numbers of verbal stimuli, and subsequent learning about the complex processes of learning are discussed in the

.

The rule used for representing the learning curve effect states that the more times a task has been performed, the less time will be required on each subsequent iteration.

a. Distribution
b. Spatial Decision Support Systems
c. Models
d. Point biserial correlation coefficient

2. _________ is an advertisement in which a particular product specifically mentions a competitor by name for the express purpose of showing why the competitor is inferior to the product naming it.

This should not be confused with parody advertisements, where a fictional product is being advertised for the purpose of poking fun at the particular advertisement, nor should it be confused with the use of a coined brand name for the purpose of comparing the product without actually naming an actual competitor. ('Wikipedia tastes better and is less filling than the Encyclopedia Galactica.')

In the 1980s, during what has been referred to as the cola wars, soft-drink manufacturer Pepsi ran a series of advertisements where people, caught on hidden camera, in a blind taste test, chose Pepsi over rival Coca-Cola.

a. 33 Strategies of War
b. Comparative advertising
c. 1990 Clean Air Act
d. 28-hour day

3. The term '_________' refers to the concept of collecting information and attempting to spot a pattern in the information. In some fields of study, the term '_________' has more formally-defined meanings.

In project management _________ is a mathematical technique that uses historical results to predict future outcome.

a. Stepwise regression
b. Least squares
c. Regression analysis
d. Trend analysis

4. Procter is a surname, and may also refer to:

- Bryan Waller Procter (pseud. Barry Cornwall), English poet
- Goodwin Procter, American law firm
- _________, consumer products multinational

a. Strict liability
b. Master and Servant Acts
c. Downstream
d. Procter ' Gamble

5. _________ is the process of estimation in unknown situations. Prediction is a similar, but more general term. Both can refer to estimation of time series, cross-sectional or longitudinal data.

a. 1990 Clean Air Act
b. 28-hour day
c. Forecasting
d. 33 Strategies of War

6. _________ is the process of comparing the cost, cycle time, productivity, or quality of a specific process or method to another that is widely considered to be an industry standard or best practice. Essentially, _________ provides a snapshot of the performance of your business and helps you understand where you are in relation to a particular standard. The result is often a business case for making changes in order to make improvements.

a. Complementors
b. Competitive heterogeneity
c. Benchmarking
d. Cost leadership

7. _________ is a term developed by Eric von Hippel in 1986. His definition for _________ is:

1. _________s face needs that will be general in a marketplace - but face them months or years before the bulk of that marketplace encounters them, and
2. _________s are positioned to benefit significantly by obtaining a solution to those needs.

In other words: _________s are users of a product that currently experience needs still unknown to the public and who also benefit greatly if they obtain a solution to these needs.

The _________ Method is a market research tool that may be used by companies and / or individuals seeking to develop breakthrough products. _________ methodology was originally developed by Dr. Eric von Hippel of the Massachusetts Institute of Technology (MIT) and first described in the July 1986 issue of the Journal of Management Science.

a. 1990 Clean Air Act
b. 28-hour day
c. 33 Strategies of War
d. Lead user

8. A _________ is an entity formed between two or more parties to undertake economic activity together. The parties agree to create a new entity by both contributing equity, and they then share in the revenues, expenses, and control of the enterprise. The venture can be for one specific project only, or a continuing business relationship such as the Fuji Xerox _________.

a. Patent
b. Meritor Savings Bank v. Vinson
c. Joint venture
d. Civil Rights Act of 1991

9. An _________ is a person who has possession of an enterprise and assumes significant accountability for the inherent risks and the outcome. It is an ambitious leader who combines land, labor, and capital to create and market new goods or services. The term is a loanword from French and was first defined by the Irish economist Richard Cantillon.

a. AAAI
b. Entrepreneur
c. A Stake in the Outcome
d. A4e

10. _________ or lean production, which is often known simply as 'Lean', is a production practice that considers the expenditure of resources for any goal other than the creation of value for the end customer to be wasteful, and thus a target for elimination. Working from the perspective of the customer who consumes a product or service, 'value' is defined as any action or process that a customer would be willing to pay for. Basically, lean is centered around creating more value with less work.

a. Theory of constraints
b. Six Sigma
c. Production line
d. Lean manufacturing

11. A _________ system is a manufacturing system in which there is some amount of flexibility that allows the system to react in the case of changes, whether predicted or unpredicted. This flexibility is generally considered to fall into two categories, which both contain numerous subcategories.

The first category, machine flexibility, covers the system's ability to be changed to produce new product types, and ability to change the order of operations executed on a part. The second category is called routing flexibility, which consists of the ability to use multiple machines to perform the same operation on a part, as well as the system's ability to absorb large-scale changes, such as in volume, capacity, or capability.

a. Jidoka
b. Manufacturing resource planning
c. Homeworkers
d. Flexible manufacturing

12. A _________ is a form of qualitative research in which a group of people are asked about their attitude towards a product, service, concept, advertisement, idea, or packaging. Questions are asked in an interactive group setting where participants are free to talk with other group members.

The first _________s were created at the Bureau of Applied Social Research by associate director, sociologist Robert K. Merton.

a. Market analysis
b. 1990 Clean Air Act
c. Marketing research
d. Focus group

13. A _________ is an alliance among individuals or groups, during which they cooperate in joint action, each in his own self-interest, joining forces together for a common cause. This alliance may be temporary or a matter of convenience. A _________ thus differs from a more formal covenant.

a. 1990 Clean Air Act
b. 28-hour day
c. 33 Strategies of War
d. Coalition

14. The phrase mergers and _________s refers to the aspect of corporate strategy, corporate finance and management dealing with the buying, selling and combining of different companies that can aid, finance, or help a growing company in a given industry grow rapidly without having to create another business entity.

An _________, also known as a takeover or a buyout, is the buying of one company (the 'target') by another. An _________ may be friendly or hostile.

a. Acquisition
b. A4e
c. AAAI
d. A Stake in the Outcome

15. _________, in marketing, manufacturing, call centres and management, is the use of flexible computer-aided manufacturing systems to produce custom output. Those systems combine the low unit costs of mass production processes with the flexibility of individual customization.

'_________' is the new frontier in business competition for both manufacturing and service industries.

a. 28-hour day
b. 1990 Clean Air Act
c. 33 Strategies of War
d. Mass customization

16. In commerce, _________ is the length of time it takes from a product being conceived until its being available for sale. _________ is important in industries where products are outmoded quickly. A common assumption is that _________ matters most for first-of-a-kind products, but actually the leader often has the luxury of time, while the clock is clearly running for the followers.

a. Time to market
b. Career development
c. Market entry
d. Procurement

17. A _________ researches, selects, develops, and places a company's products.

A _________ considers numerous factors such as target demographic, the products offered by the competition, and how well the product fits in with the company's business model. Generally, a _________ manages one or more tangible products.

a. 1990 Clean Air Act
b. Product manager
c. 28-hour day
d. 33 Strategies of War

18. _________ is an integrated communications-based process through which individuals and communities discover that existing and newly-identified needs and wants may be satisfied by the products and services of others.

_________ is defined by the American _________ Association as the activity, set of institutions, and processes for creating, communicating, delivering, and exchanging offerings that have value for customers, clients, partners, and society at large. The term developed from the original meaning which referred literally to going to market, as in shopping, or going to a market to buy or sell goods or services.

a. Disruptive technology
b. Market development
c. Customer relationship management
d. Marketing

19. A _________, in the field of business and marketing, is a geographic region or demographic group used to gauge the viability of a product or service in the mass market prior to a wide scale roll-out. The criteria used to judge the acceptability of a _________ region or group include:

1. a population that is demographically similar to the proposed target market; and
2. relative isolation from densely populated media markets so that advertising to the test audience can be efficient and economical.

The _________ ideally aims to duplicate 'everything' - promotion and distribution as well as `product' - on a smaller scale. The technique replicates, typically in one area, what is planned to occur in a national launch; and the results are very carefully monitored, so that they can be extrapolated to projected national results. The `area' may be any one of the following:

- Television area

internet online test

- Test town
- Residential neighborhood
- Test site

A number of decisions have to be taken about any _________:

- Which _________?
- What is to be tested?
- How long a test?
- What are the success criteria?

The simple go or no-go decision, together with the related reduction of risk, is normally the main justification for the expense of _________s. At the same time, however, such _________s can be used to test specific elements of a new product's marketing mix; possibly the version of the product itself, the promotional message and media spend, the distribution channels and the price.

a. 33 Strategies of War
b. 1990 Clean Air Act
c. Test market
d. 28-hour day

20. The _________ is generally accepted as the use and specification of the 'four P's' describing the strategic position of a product in the marketplace. One version of the _________ originated in 1948 when James Culliton said that a marketing decision should be a result of something similar to a recipe. This version was used in 1953 when Neil Borden, in his American Marketing Association presidential address, took the recipe idea one step further and coined the term 'marketing-mix'.

a. 33 Strategies of War
b. 1990 Clean Air Act
c. 28-hour day
d. Marketing mix

21. A _________ is a written document that details the necessary actions to achieve one or more marketing objectives. It can be for a product or service, a brand, or a product line. _________s cover between one and five years.

a. Disruptive technology
b. Market development
c. Marketing strategy
d. Marketing plan

22. _________ is a structured approach to transitioning individuals, teams, and organizations from a current state to a desired future state. The current definition of _________ includes both organizational _________ processes and individual _________ models, which together are used to manage the people side of change.

A number of models are available for understanding the transitioning of individuals through the phases of _________ and strengthening organizational development initiative in both government and corporate sectors.

a. 1990 Clean Air Act
b. 33 Strategies of War
c. 28-hour day
d. Change management

23. _________ is, in very basic words, a position a firm occupies against its competitors.

According to Michael Porter, the three methods for creating a sustainable _________ are through:

1. Cost leadership

2. Differentiation

3. Focus (economics)

a. 1990 Clean Air Act
b. Theory Z
c. 28-hour day
d. Competitive advantage

24. _________ is an uncomfortable feeling caused by holding two contradictory ideas simultaneously. The 'ideas' or 'cognitions' in question may include attitudes and beliefs, and also the awareness of one's behavior. The theory of _________ proposes that people have a motivational drive to reduce dissonance by changing their attitudes, beliefs, and behaviors, or by justifying or rationalizing their attitudes, beliefs, and behaviors.

a. Quantitative psychology
b. Cognitive bias
c. Trait theory
d. Cognitive dissonance

1. An _________ is a person who has possession of an enterprise and assumes significant accountability for the inherent risks and the outcome. It is an ambitious leader who combines land, labor, and capital to create and market new goods or services. The term is a loanword from French and was first defined by the Irish economist Richard Cantillon.
a. AAAI
b. Entrepreneur
c. A Stake in the Outcome
d. A4e

2. _________ according to Onuoha (2007) is the practice of starting new organizations or revitalizing mature organizations, particularly new businesses generally in response to identified opportunities. _________ is often a difficult undertaking, as a vast majority of new businesses fail. Entrepreneurial activities are substantially different depending on the type of organization that is being started.
a. A4e
b. AAAI
c. A Stake in the Outcome
d. Entrepreneurship

3. In business and engineering, _________ is the term used to describe the complete process of bringing a new product or service to market. There are two parallel paths involved in the _________ process: one involves the idea generation, product design, and detail engineering; the other involves market research and marketing analysis. Companies typically see _________ as the first stage in generating and commercializing new products within the overall strategic process of product life cycle management used to maintain or grow their market share.
a. 28-hour day
b. 1990 Clean Air Act
c. 33 Strategies of War
d. New product development

4. In business and engineering, new _________ is the term used to describe the complete process of bringing a new product or service to market. There are two parallel paths involved in the NProduct development process: one involves the idea generation, product design, and detail engineering; the other involves market research and marketing analysis. Companies typically see new _________ as the first stage in generating and commercializing new products within the overall strategic process of product life cycle management used to maintain or grow their market share.
a. 28-hour day
b. 1990 Clean Air Act
c. Product development
d. 33 Strategies of War

5. _________ is a type of private equity capital typically provided to early-stage, high-potential, growth companies in the interest of generating a return through an eventual realization event such as an IPO or trade sale of the company. _________ investments are generally made as cash in exchange for shares in the invested company. It is typical for _________ investors to identify and back companies in high technology industries such as biotechnology and ICT.

a. Limited liability corporation
b. Seed round
c. Private equity
d. Venture capital

6. _________ is the process by which a new idea or new product is accepted by the market. The rate of _________ is the speed that the new idea spreads from one consumer to the next. Adoption is similar to _________ except that it deals with the psychological processes an individual goes through, rather than an aggregate market process.

a. Value chain
b. Mass marketing
c. Diffusion
d. Category management

7. An _________ is a private computer network that uses Internet technologies to securely share any part of an organization's information or operational systems with its employees. Sometimes the term refers only to the organization's internal website, but often it is a more extensive part of the organization's computer infrastructure and private websites are an important component and focal point of internal communication and collaboration.

An _________ is built from the same concepts and technologies used for the Internet, such as client-server computing and the Internet Protocol Suite (TCP/IP.)

a. AAAI
b. A Stake in the Outcome
c. Intranet
d. A4e

8. A _________ is a formal statement of a set of business goals, the reasons why they are believed attainable, and the plan for reaching those goals. It may also contain background information about the organization or team attempting to reach those goals.

The business goals may be defined for for-profit or for non-profit organizations.

a. Distributed management
b. Crisis management
c. Time management
d. Business plan

9. In decision theory and estimation theory, the _________ of an estimator, $\hat{\theta}$, of an unknown parameter of the distribution, θ, is the expected value of the loss function

$$R(\theta,\hat{\theta}) = \mathbb{E}_\theta L(\theta,\hat{\theta}) = \int L(\theta,\hat{\theta})\, dP_\theta.$$

where dP_θ is a probability measure parametrized by θ.

- For a scalar parameter θ and a quadratic loss function,

  $$L(\theta,\hat{\theta}) = (\theta - \hat{\theta})^2$$

  the _________ function becomes the mean squared error of the estimate,

  $$R(\theta,\hat{\theta}) = E_\theta(\theta - \hat{\theta})^2$$

- In density estimation, the unknown parameter is probability density itself. The loss function is typically chosen to be a norm in an appropriate function space. For example, for L^2 norm,

  $$L(f,\hat{f}) = \|f - \hat{f}\|_2^2$$

  the _________ function becomes the mean integrated squared error

  $$R(f,\hat{f}) = E\|f - \hat{f}\|^2$$

.

a. Risk aversion
b. Risk
c. Linear model
d. Financial modeling

10. In finance and economics, _________ or divestiture is the reduction of some kind of asset for either financial or ethical objectives or sale of an existing business by a firm. A _________ is the opposite of an investment.

a. 33 Strategies of War
b. 28-hour day
c. 1990 Clean Air Act
d. Divestment

11. A _________ is a new organization or entity formed by a split from a larger one, such as a television series based on a pre-existing one, or a new company formed from a university research group or business incubator. In literature, especially in milieu-based popular fictional book series like mysteries, westerns, fantasy or science fiction, the term sub-series is generally used instead of _________, but with essentially the same meaning.

_________s as a descriptive term can also include a dissenting faction of a membership organization, a sect of a cult, or a denomination of a church.

a. 33 Strategies of War
b. 1990 Clean Air Act
c. Spin-off
d. 28-hour day

12. A _________ is a set of exclusive rights granted by a state to an inventor or his assignee for a limited period of time in exchange for a disclosure of an invention.

The procedure for granting _________s, the requirements placed on the _________ee and the extent of the exclusive rights vary widely between countries according to national laws and international agreements. Typically, however, a _________ application must include one or more claims defining the invention which must be new, inventive, and useful or industrially applicable.

a. Labor Management Reporting and Disclosure Act
b. Federal Trade Commission Act
c. Food, Drug, and Cosmetic Act
d. Patent

1. _________ has been described as the 'process of social influence in which one person can enlist the aid and support of others in the accomplishment of a common task' . A definition more inclusive of followers comes from Alan Keith of Genentech who said '_________ is ultimately about creating a way for people to contribute to making something extraordinary happen.'

_________ is one of the most salient aspects of the organizational context. However, defining _________ has been challenging.

a. 28-hour day
b. Situational leadership
c. 1990 Clean Air Act
d. Leadership

2. _________ is technology based on biology, especially when used in agriculture, food science, and medicine. United Nations Convention on Biological Diversity defines _________ as:

_________ is often used to refer to genetic engineering technology of the 21st century, however the term encompasses a wider range and history of procedures for modifying biological organisms according to the needs of humanity, going back to the initial modifications of native plants into improved food crops through artificial selection and hybridization. Bioengineering is the science upon which all biotechnological applications are based.

a. Biotechnology
b. 1990 Clean Air Act
c. 28-hour day
d. 33 Strategies of War

3. _________ or lean production, which is often known simply as 'Lean', is a production practice that considers the expenditure of resources for any goal other than the creation of value for the end customer to be wasteful, and thus a target for elimination. Working from the perspective of the customer who consumes a product or service, 'value' is defined as any action or process that a customer would be willing to pay for. Basically, lean is centered around creating more value with less work.

a. Production line
b. Six Sigma
c. Theory of constraints
d. Lean manufacturing

4. _________ is the production of large amounts of standardized products, including and especially on assembly lines. The concepts of _________ are applied to various kinds of products, from fluids and particulates handled in bulk to discrete solid parts to assemblies of such parts

_________ of assemblies typically uses electric-motor-powered moving tracks or conveyor belts to move partially complete products to workers, who perform simple repetitive tasks.

a. 33 Strategies of War
b. 28-hour day
c. 1990 Clean Air Act
d. Mass production

5. _________ is a theory of management that analyzes and synthesizes workflows, with the objective of improving labour productivity. The core ideas of the theory were developed by Frederick Winslow Taylor in the 1880s and 1890s, and were first published in his monographs, Shop Management and The Principles of _________ Taylor believed that decisions based upon tradition and rules of thumb should be replaced by precise procedures developed after careful study of an individual at work.
a. Master production schedule
b. Capacity planning
c. Scientific management
d. Value engineering

6. In probability theory, a probability distribution is called _________ if its cumulative distribution function is _________. This is equivalent to saying that for random variables X with the distribution in question, Pr[X = a] = 0 for all real numbers a, i.e.: the probability that X attains the value a is zero, for any number a. If the distribution of X is _________ then X is called a _________ random variable.
a. Decision tree pruning
b. Pay Band
c. Connectionist expert systems
d. Continuous

7. _________ is a management process whereby delivery (customer valued) processes are constantly evaluated and improved in the light of their efficiency, effectiveness and flexibility.

Some see it as a meta process for most management systems (Business Process Management, Quality Management, Project Management). Deming saw it as part of the 'system' whereby feedback from the process and customer were evaluated against organisational goals.

a. Critical Success Factor
b. First-mover advantage
c. Sole proprietorship
d. Continuous Improvement Process

8. A _________ is an entity formed between two or more parties to undertake economic activity together. The parties agree to create a new entity by both contributing equity, and they then share in the revenues, expenses, and control of the enterprise. The venture can be for one specific project only, or a continuing business relationship such as the Fuji Xerox _________.
a. Joint venture
b. Civil Rights Act of 1991
c. Patent
d. Meritor Savings Bank v. Vinson

9. An _________ is a person who has possession of an enterprise and assumes significant accountability for the inherent risks and the outcome. It is an ambitious leader who combines land, labor, and capital to create and market new goods or services. The term is a loanword from French and was first defined by the Irish economist Richard Cantillon.
a. Entrepreneur
b. A4e
c. AAAI
d. A Stake in the Outcome

10. _________ can be considered to have three main components: quality control, quality assurance and quality improvement. _________ is focused not only on product quality, but also the means to achieve it. _________ therefore uses quality assurance and control of processes as well as products to achieve more consistent quality.
a. Total quality management
b. 28-hour day
c. 1990 Clean Air Act
d. Quality management

11. _________ is a recursive process where two or more people or organizations work together in an intersection of common goals -- for example, an intellectual endeavor that is creative in nature--by sharing knowledge, learning and building consensus. _________ does not require leadership and can sometimes bring better results through decentralization and egalitarianism. In particular, teams that work collaboratively can obtain greater resources, recognition and reward when facing competition for finite resources._________ is also present in opposing goals exhibiting the notion of adversarial _________, though this is not a common case for using the term.

a. Collectivism
b. 28-hour day
c. 1990 Clean Air Act
d. Collaboration

12. _________ is the discipline of managing processes in research and development (R'D) and innovation. It can be used to develop both product and organizational innovation. Without proper processes, it is not possible for R'D to be efficient; _________ includes a set of tools that allow managers and engineers to cooperate with a common understanding of goals and processes.
a. A4e
b. A Stake in the Outcome
c. AAAI
d. Innovation management

1. A _________ is a set of exclusive rights granted by a state to an inventor or his assignee for a limited period of time in exchange for a disclosure of an invention.

The procedure for granting _________s, the requirements placed on the _________ee and the extent of the exclusive rights vary widely between countries according to national laws and international agreements. Typically, however, a _________ application must include one or more claims defining the invention which must be new, inventive, and useful or industrially applicable.

a. Patent
b. Federal Trade Commission Act
c. Food, Drug, and Cosmetic Act
d. Labor Management Reporting and Disclosure Act

2. _________ according to Onuoha (2007) is the practice of starting new organizations or revitalizing mature organizations, particularly new businesses generally in response to identified opportunities. _________ is often a difficult undertaking, as a vast majority of new businesses fail. Entrepreneurial activities are substantially different depending on the type of organization that is being started.

a. A4e
b. Entrepreneurship
c. A Stake in the Outcome
d. AAAI

3. In decision theory and estimation theory, the _________ of an estimator, $\hat{\theta}$, of an unknown parameter of the distribution, θ, is the expected value of the loss function

$$R(\theta,\hat{\theta}) = \mathbb{E}_\theta L(\theta,\hat{\theta}) = \int L(\theta,\hat{\theta})\,dP_\theta.$$

where dP_θ is a probability measure parametrized by θ.

- For a scalar parameter θ and a quadratic loss function,

  $$L(\theta,\hat{\theta}) = (\theta - \hat{\theta})^2$$

  the _________ function becomes the mean squared error of the estimate,

  $$R(\theta,\hat{\theta}) = E_\theta(\theta - \hat{\theta})^2$$

- In density estimation, the unknown parameter is probability density itself. The loss function is typically chosen to be a norm in an appropriate function space. For example, for L^2 norm,

  $$L(f,\hat{f}) = \|f - \hat{f}\|_2^2$$

  the _________ function becomes the mean integrated squared error

  $$R(f,\hat{f}) = E\|f - \hat{f}\|^2$$

.

a. Risk
b. Financial modeling
c. Risk aversion
d. Linear model

4. _________ is technology based on biology, especially when used in agriculture, food science, and medicine. United Nations Convention on Biological Diversity defines _________ as:

_________ is often used to refer to genetic engineering technology of the 21st century, however the term encompasses a wider range and history of procedures for modifying biological organisms according to the needs of humanity, going back to the initial modifications of native plants into improved food crops through artificial selection and hybridization. Bioengineering is the science upon which all biotechnological applications are based.

a. 1990 Clean Air Act
b. 33 Strategies of War
c. 28-hour day
d. Biotechnology

5. A _________ is a formal statement of a set of business goals, the reasons why they are believed attainable, and the plan for reaching those goals. It may also contain background information about the organization or team attempting to reach those goals.

The business goals may be defined for for-profit or for non-profit organizations.

a. Crisis management
b. Time management
c. Distributed management
d. Business plan

6. An _________ is a person who has possession of an enterprise and assumes significant accountability for the inherent risks and the outcome. It is an ambitious leader who combines land, labor, and capital to create and market new goods or services. The term is a loanword from French and was first defined by the Irish economist Richard Cantillon.

a. AAAI
b. Entrepreneur
c. A Stake in the Outcome
d. A4e

7. _________ is a type of private equity capital typically provided to early-stage, high-potential, growth companies in the interest of generating a return through an eventual realization event such as an IPO or trade sale of the company. _________ investments are generally made as cash in exchange for shares in the invested company. It is typical for _________ investors to identify and back companies in high technology industries such as biotechnology and ICT.

a. Venture capital
b. Limited liability corporation
c. Private equity
d. Seed round

8. An _________ is a private computer network that uses Internet technologies to securely share any part of an organization's information or operational systems with its employees. Sometimes the term refers only to the organization's internal website, but often it is a more extensive part of the organization's computer infrastructure and private websites are an important component and focal point of internal communication and collaboration.

An _________ is built from the same concepts and technologies used for the Internet, such as client-server computing and the Internet Protocol Suite (TCP/IP.)

a. AAAI
b. Intranet
c. A Stake in the Outcome
d. A4e

1. _________ is the process of comparing the cost, cycle time, productivity, or quality of a specific process or method to another that is widely considered to be an industry standard or best practice. Essentially, _________ provides a snapshot of the performance of your business and helps you understand where you are in relation to a particular standard. The result is often a business case for making changes in order to make improvements.

a. Complementors
b. Benchmarking
c. Cost leadership
d. Competitive heterogeneity

2. _________ can be considered to have three main components: quality control, quality assurance and quality improvement. _________ is focused not only on product quality, but also the means to achieve it. _________ therefore uses quality assurance and control of processes as well as products to achieve more consistent quality.

a. 1990 Clean Air Act
b. 28-hour day
c. Total quality management
d. Quality management

3. A _________ is a set of exclusive rights granted by a state to an inventor or his assignee for a limited period of time in exchange for a disclosure of an invention.

The procedure for granting _________s, the requirements placed on the _________ee and the extent of the exclusive rights vary widely between countries according to national laws and international agreements. Typically, however, a _________ application must include one or more claims defining the invention which must be new, inventive, and useful or industrially applicable.

a. Federal Trade Commission Act
b. Labor Management Reporting and Disclosure Act
c. Food, Drug, and Cosmetic Act
d. Patent

Chapter 1

1. c 2. d 3. c 4. c 5. a 6. a 7. c 8. d 9. d 10. d
11. d

Chapter 2

1. d 2. c 3. c 4. d 5. d 6. d 7. d 8. d 9. d 10. b
11. a

Chapter 3

1. d 2. d 3. b 4. d 5. d

Chapter 4

1. a 2. a 3. a 4. c 5. d 6. d 7. d 8. d 9. c 10. b
11. d 12. d 13. b

Chapter 5

1. c 2. b 3. c 4. d 5. d 6. d

Chapter 6

1. d 2. d 3. b 4. a 5. b 6. c 7. c 8. a 9. d

Chapter 7

1. c 2. d 3. b 4. a 5. d 6. d 7. d 8. d 9. d 10. c
11. c 12. b 13. d 14. d 15. d 16. a 17. c 18. d 19. d

Chapter 8

1. d 2. c 3. b 4. d 5. d 6. d 7. c 8. d 9. d 10. b
11. c 12. a 13. d 14. c

Chapter 9

1. c 2. b 3. d 4. d 5. c 6. c 7. d 8. c 9. b 10. d
11. d 12. d 13. d 14. a 15. d 16. a 17. b 18. d 19. c 20. d
21. d 22. d 23. d 24. d

Chapter 10

1. b 2. d 3. d 4. c 5. d 6. c 7. c 8. d 9. b 10. d
11. c 12. d

Chapter 11

1. d 2. a 3. d 4. d 5. c 6. d 7. d 8. a 9. a 10. d
11. d 12. d

Chapter 12

1. a 2. b 3. a 4. d 5. d 6. b 7. a 8. b

Chapter 13

1. b 2. d 3. d

www.ingramcontent.com/pod-product-compliance
Lightning Source LLC
Chambersburg PA
CBHW080744250426
43671CB00038B/2858
9781428872967